Into My Magical World

Celine Joan

DEDICATION

This book is dedicated to my parents, who have always encouraged me to pursue my dreams and supported me in every step of the way. Without their love and guidance, I would not be where I am today.

To all the readers out there, young and old. Thank you for giving my stories a chance to come alive in your imagination. This book is for all of you, with my heartfelt gratitude.

Sincerely,
Celine Joan

CONTENTS

ACKNOWLEDGMENTS

I would like to express my heartfelt gratitude to all the people who have supported me throughout this writing journey.

First and foremost, I am deeply grateful to my parents for their unwavering love, encouragement, and patience. They have been my constant source of inspiration, and I couldn't have done this without them.

I would like to thank my editor, Celestine, my father, for his invaluable feedback, guidance, and support. His expertise and dedication to this project have helped me to bring my vision to life.

Finally, I would like to express my gratitude to all the readers who have embraced my work and supported me along the way. Your enthusiasm and encouragement have meant the world to me, and I am humbled and grateful for your support.

Sincerely,

Celine Joan

SUZY'S TALKING DOG

Suzy was a little girl who had a dog named Rover. One day, she was playing fetch with Rover. Suzy threw the ball little far away by mistake. She heard someone ask, "Where is the ball?" Suzy was puzzled!

She looked around and found none – Mysterious. She again heard the same words, "Where is the ball?". This time, she suspected that Rover is saying that and realized Rover is really saying something to her.

Suzy told her parents about Rover speaking, but her parents didn't believe her. Again, she heard Rover saying, "I want to go to the slide ride in the back yard. Pretty please...." Rover went to the back yard with Suzy, climbed on the slide and came down saying, "Wee!"

Suzy had another ball in her pocket. She threw the ball far away. Rover said, "Suzy, all blames on you" This time Suzy has set her parents around to watch Rover speak. Her parents were astonished to know that Rover is speaking.

They trusted Suzy and from that day, they all talk to Rover and he was treated just like a brother to Suzy. They had lot of fun everyday playing with Rover. From that day onwards, magical Rover talks to the family for anything and everything instead of barking.

MAX's CAMPING ADVENTURE

Max and his family were planning to go camping in a dark jungle to spend time with nature and see animals. As soon as, Max and his family entered the jungle, Max said to mom and dad," I feel very scared." Max started to cry. Dad said, "Max, there's nothing to be scared of because we are here." Max cheered up and walked along dad.

They went deep into the jungle and it was about to darken. Max said, "Mom, I feel hungry." Mom roasted some marshmallows and gave it to Max.

After Max ate it, his dad called him and said," Son, look… it is a deer." "Wow it is so pretty." Max said. "You two, come inside the tent, it is almost dark," Mom said. Max and his family snuggled into their sleeping bags.

There was a loud bird hooting that woke up dad. Dad shook Max and said," Mom is missing!" Max frightfully said, "What!" Dad said, " Max, we got to find mom."

They both took their emergency flash lights and started their search. Max whispered, "Dad, I can hear a voice which says help me!" "Oh, look dad, there is a big bird on the tree and I can see mom over there."

Dad said, " Let's go and save mom, are you with me?" " Yes!" said Max. "Climb on my back and let's climb that tree." said Dad. After they climbed up to the tree, as they reached where they saw mom, the bird moved further up. Dad grabbed a stick and scared the bird off the tree and heroically saved mom.

Then they climbed down the tree and the bird was chasing after them, they ran faster and faster to reach their tent and by the time, it became dawn and the bird disappeared. Ah! a sigh of relief... They packed their things and went back home safely. Max told all about the adventure they had in the jungle to his friends in his neighborhood.

THE LONELY BABY JINGO, THE ELEPHANT

There was a forest where animals always played happily except for a lonely baby elephant named Jingo. One day, Jingo was walking in the forest in search of food. He found a banana tree and ate the bananas. As he ate, he thought that he can go and find new friends. After he was done eating, he went to find new friends with hope.

As Jingo walked in the forest, he saw two monkeys.

Jingo asked, "Hey monkeys, can I be your friend?" The monkey "Sorry, you're too big." Jingo still did not lose hope so he continued walking. Then he saw a mouse. Jingo asked," Can I be your friend?" The mouse ran away with fear.

Jingo continued walking…

Then Jingo saw a rabbit and asked, "Will you be my friend?" The rabbit said, "You cannot be my friend because you may not be able to run as fast as me." Then Jingo lost hope and walked back home with disappointment.

On the way back home, Jingo noticed all the animals were terrified and running in the opposite direction.

Jingo stopped a rabbit and asked, "Why are you all running?"

The rabbit said, "The tiger, Liress has come to eat us so we are finding a place to hide and you go find a place to hide too." Jingo said, "All of you get to safety and I will fight Liress."

Jingo and Liress the angry tiger met face-to-face.

Liress said, "I will eat you; you are a baby elephant and you can't fight me."

Jingo said, "I am here and I am ready to fight, let us see who is strong". "I will see about that now, fight me.", said Liress.

Liress pounced on Jingo but Jingo punched on Liress' face and belly. Liress became tired and said, "Okay, okay you win baby elephant", and Liress ran away.

After Liress ran away, Jingo said that Liress is gone so you all can come out now

and have fun. All the animals were happy about this and thanked

Jingo for saving them.

From that day onwards, the rabbit, mouse, Jingo and the two monkeys became friends and Jingo realized that he is not lonely anymore.

They all had fun and lived happily together as best friends ever.

THE DANCING FROG

Once upon a time, there was a small village with all sorts of animals. They were always happiness and there was no sorrow. If there was sorrow, they will call upon the one and only dancing frog.

Now, this frog has been in deep sleep for many years. In that village, there was a leader who became really tired and miserable. His servant was so terrified to see his leader so unhappy.

The leader summoned, " Call upon the one and only dancing frog."

The servant went to an enchanted place and chanted the words, " Frog, froggy, frog, we need your power to solve."

The frog woke up and said, " At your service, servant." The servant brought the dancing frog to the leader. The frog asked, " So, what is the problem here? Wait what did I just say."

The frog then came to know that the leader was sick. The frog felt bad about the leader's situation and opened a bag he had and said, " Let us see what we can do."

He took a radio and a tutu out of his bag. He wore it and switched on the radio. He started doing some ballet moves and purposefully messed up. Then he did a split at the end and said, " Ow!" That made the servant laugh but not the leader.

The frog the said, " What can I do?" The frog kept thinking about what can be done.

The frog then did the tap dance. He moved his neck sideways and then kept on saying oooah, oooah. That made the leader laugh so much that his sickness was gone and it was time for the frog to leave.

The frog set his journey back to his home. On the way home, everyone started yelling, " Run, ah, monster, run!"

The frog saw the monster and said, " Hey, you! You don't scare my people; um I mean the leader's people." The monster started to laugh for no reason in the frog's point of view but in others point of view, it was really funny because the frog was dancing.

The monster laughed so much that he started turning into salt! The frog started sitting on it and asked, " Who wants free salt or sugar? I don't know whether it is salt or sugar."

All the people started carrying bags of salt. The frog still did not know whether the white powder was salt or sugar. He wanted to try it and he always knew things happen in contrary to what he thinks.

He was determined that he would be tasting sugar and not salt.

He took some of the powder in his fingers and then licked with his lipstick pink tongue. He tasted salt and was really looking so ridiculous indeed. He had a bitter expression on his face which again made everyone laugh. The frog then asked, " What's so funny? Ribbit"

If he does the ribbit sound three more times, he will end up in a place which he hates. The human world.

He said that he would better go back to his sleep rather than getting into trouble that he really deserves. He hopped back to his home and went back to sleep. He was in a world called wonderland for frogs only, no trespassers allowed.

With the complete satisfaction of solving the leader's problem, the frog went back to its long sleep.

THE NAUGHTY MOUSE

Once there lived two kittens and they loved playing together. They used to go around everywhere together. One day the kittens saw some food and one of the kittens said, "I will eat the food first."

The other kitten exclaimed, "No, I will eat it first." Then, they both started arguing and fighting.

In the meantime, a mouse came by and asked, "Why are you both fighting?"

They said, "We are arguing about who can eat the food first."
The mouse said, "I can solve this problem..."

For that, you need to close your eyes for a few seconds". The kittens agreed and thanked the mouse for jumping into the situation to solve

the problem and closed their eyes hopefully.

As soon as the kittens closed their eyes, the mouse ate the whole food. Then the mouse said, "Tadaaa... you can open your eyes now", and ran away.

The kittens opened their eyes and were shocked by looking at what happened. They said, "Our food is eaten by the mouse".

The kittens were disappointed and went back home sadly.

Both the kittens realized that they should have thought about sharing the food, and they would have had the food instead of losing it to the naughty mouse.

THE GREEDY MAN

There was a man who was always crazy about being so rich and wanted lots of gold. One day the man was going for a walk in the woods.

While he was walking, he saw a fairy. The fairy asked the man, "What do you wish for?"

The man said, "I wish I had a golden touch". The fairy said, "Your wish is my command" Then the fairy gave the man the golden touch.

The man went back home, and when he opened the door, the door turned into gold. The man was delighted. He felt hungry and grabbed an apple, that apple also turned into gold. He said, "This is a nightmare".

He called for the fairy and the fairy appeared. The man explained what happened to the food and door. The fairy said, "I need to take away the golden touch wish".

The man said, "Why don't you grant a wish that does not turn the food into gold?

The fairy said, "You are greedy and wishes don't work that way." Then, the fairy took away the golden touch from the man and said to the man, "For your greed you will turn into gold and never be able to come back to normal without losing the greediness from you".

Being greedy will lead us into a state of being stuck. Never be greedy!

CROSSWORD PUZZLE

Q	I	O	U	G	O	O	G	L	E	B	O	L	D	D
C	A	T	N	B	G	O	L	D	R	O	N	E	I	A
D	O	O	M	E	L	E	P	H	A	N	T	O	Z	U
A	N	D	O	A	O	P	T	I	C	D	S	U	Z	Y
D	M	O	U	N	W	J	R	K	V	I	O	L	A	H
F	M	G	S	B	I	U	O	I	I	L	L	A	B	E
A	A	C	E	A	N	N	M	T	O	A	E	R	G	A
D	X	L	A	G	G	G	B	T	L	E	V	I	R	D
E	I	I	G	A	L	L	O	E	I	L	A	U	G	H
D	M	M	A	D	O	E	N	N	N	H	A	P	P	Y
H	J	I	N	G	O	Y	E	S	C	E	L	L	O	E
O	U	T	E	R	M	G	R	E	E	D	Y	A	A	V
O	J	O	P	I	A	N	O	N	T	R	E	B	L	E
K	W	E	N	D	Y	O	B	A	S	S	E	N	T	N
S	M	E	N	D	I	N	G	G	S	I	E	N	O	T

ACROSS:

1. The color everything turned into by the greedy man's touch.

2. A girl who had a talking dog.

3. The pet that could speak in one of the stories.

4. The man's behavior that led to his lesson.

5. The baby elephant who was lonely.

DOWN:

1. A naughty animal that troubled two kittens.

2. The playful pets from the first story.

3. The boy who went on a camping adventure.

4. Where Max went camping.

5. The animal who searched for friends.

ABOUT THE AUTHOR

Celine Joan is a gifted storyteller whose remarkable ability to craft captivating tales emerged at the tender age of three.

Her passion for storytelling blossomed early, and by seven, she was penning imaginative short stories that showcased her vibrant creativity.

Celine draws inspiration from a rich tapestry of sources, including the books she devours, the animals she observes, and the intricate beauty of plants, weaving these elements into her narratives with finesse.

When not immersed in writing, Celine indulges her eclectic interests: she plays the violin with soulful precision, loses herself in the pages of a good book, sings with heartfelt melody, and competes energetically on the tennis court.